LITTLE BOOK OF

Crochet

First published in the UK in 2015

© Demand Media Limited 2015

www.demand-media.co.uk

All rights reserved. No part of this work may be reproduced or
utilised in any form or by any means, electronic or mechanical,
including photocopying, recording or by any information
storage and retrieval system, without prior written permission
of the publisher.

Printed and bound in Europe

ISBN 978-1-910540-14-5

Contents

Abbreviations...

ch	foundation chain	**ss**	slip stitch
dc	double crochet stitch	**st**	stitch
dec	decrease(ing)	**tr**	treble stitch
inc	increase(ing)	**( )**	work instructions inside the brackets as many times as instructed

Introduction

Learn to crochet with me Clare Davies - crochet teacher at The Gilliangladrag Fluff-a-torium. I like to think I'm a patient knitting and crochet teacher and I regularly hold classes in the studio. Over the coming pages, I will share with you the basics to get you started, and then move you on to some simple projects to practice what you've learnt.

You'll be crocheting in no time!

Chapter 1

The Basics
Things you'll need to crochet...

Yarns comes in lots of different thicknesses and weights. Chunky yarns crochet up faster and are warmer, whereas finer yarns can be used for delicate work but take longer to crochet.

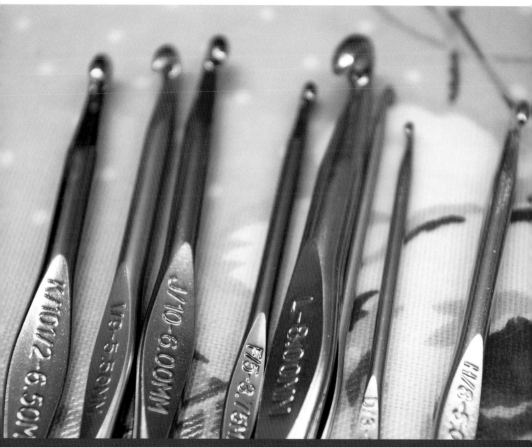

Hooks come in lots of different sizes. To work out which size you need, look at the ball band around the yarn, and the pattern.

There are lots of things that are useful to have around when crocheting, such as a tape measure, stitch markers, row counter, scissors and a tapestry needle etc.

Chapter 2

Getting Started
Making a Slipknot...

1. Make a slipknot by looping the yarn and pushing the long end through the loop.

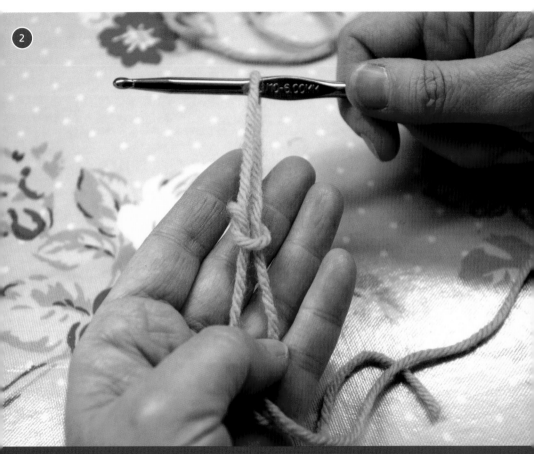

2. Push the needle into the loop you've pushed through; hold both tails –
one tail will pull the knot tight...

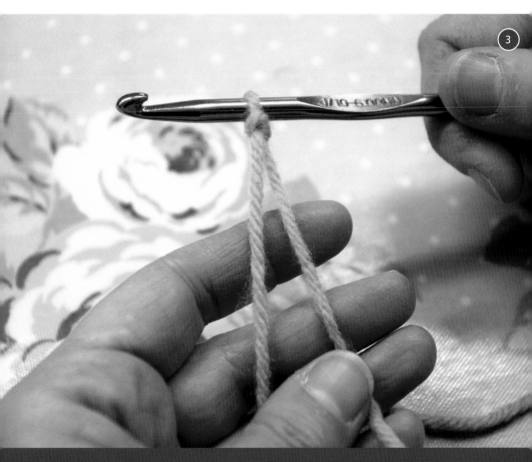

3. ...and the other tail will pull the knot up to the needle.

How to hold the yarn...

1. With your left hand pinch the knot underneath the hook.

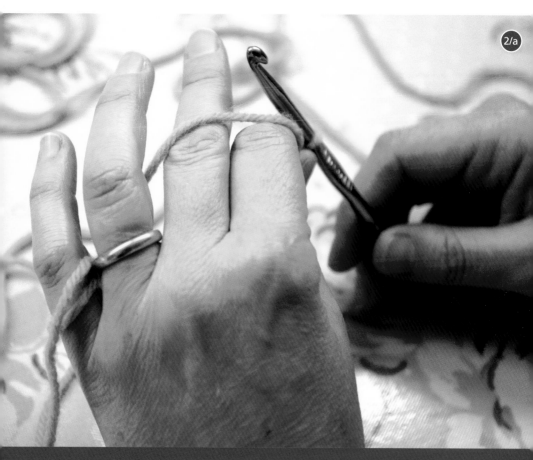

2/a. Run the yarn over your first 2 fingers, under your ring finger and round your little finger.

Making a foundation chain...

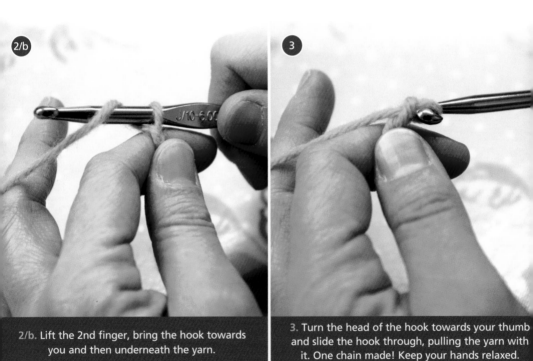

2/b. Lift the 2nd finger, bring the hook towards you and then underneath the yarn.

3. Turn the head of the hook towards your thumb and slide the hook through, pulling the yarn with it. One chain made! Keep your hands relaxed.

4

4. Continue in this way, pinching underneath the hook after each stitch, until you have a foundation chain.

Chapter 3

Different Stitches
The Double Crochet Stitch...

1. Each little "v" is a stitch. Don't count the loop on the hook, miss the first stitch, push the hook through the upper bar of the 2nd stitch.

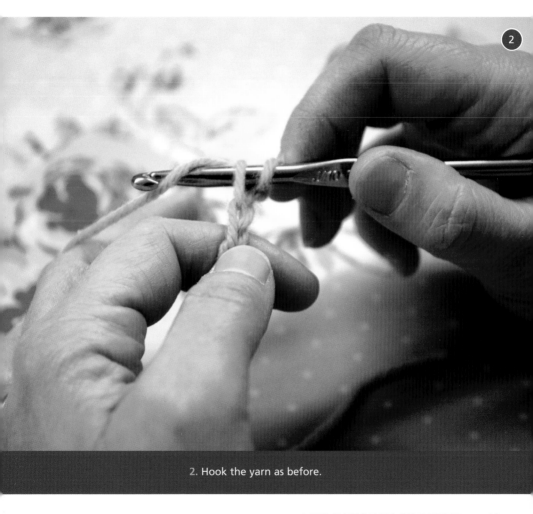

2. Hook the yarn as before.

3. **Then** pull the yarn back through the stitch (2 loops on hook).

4. Hook the yarn again in the same way.

5. Pull through the two loops on the hook. One double crochet (dc) made.

6. The worked stitch will be stretched, so avoid this and push the hook through the next stitch along.

5. Repeat to the end of the chain.

8. Flip the work over so the back is facing you, make 2 chains (turning chain).

9. Miss the 1st stitch in the row (turning chain counts as 1st stitch).
Tip the work towards you so you can see the "v" on the top of the row.

10. This time, push the hook through *both* bars of the stitch, hook the yarn and pull back as before.

11. Yarn round your hook and pull through the two loops on the hook to finish the stitch.
If you still have two loops on the hook, you haven't finished the stitch!
Fasten off your work by pulling the tail back through the last stitch worked.

Working back into the first turning chain - your 3rd row:

1. Work to the last "V" in the row, - the work will not look straight but don't worry. The turning chain doesn't have a "v " on the top, insert the hook into the top of the chain work it aswell.

Treble Stitch...

1

1. Make 3 turning chains (counts as first tr).

2. Yarn around your hook to start, push the hook into the 2nd stitch,
pull yarn back through (3 loops on hook).

3. Yarn round hook and pull through 2 of the loops.

4. Yarn round hook for a 3rd time and pull through the two loops to finish the stitch.

5. Treble stitches are taller and easier to count.

Slip Stitch...

1. Use the slip stitch to join 2 pieces of crochet together or to move the yarn to a different location. Start by inserting the hook through, (no turning chain required) hook the yarn.

2

2. Pull it through both loops.

3. Completed slip stitches.

Chapter 4

Granny Square
All same colour...

1. Chain 6 and Slip Stitch into 1st stitch to make a ring.

2. Chain 3, (acts as 1st treble), 2 more trebles through the centre of the ring, 3 chains (corner space).
Make sure you work into the centre ring only for this round.

3. Work 3 trebles into the ring, then 3 chains. Repeat until you have 4 sets of trebles and 4 sets of chains.

4. Then slip stitch into the top of the 1st treble.

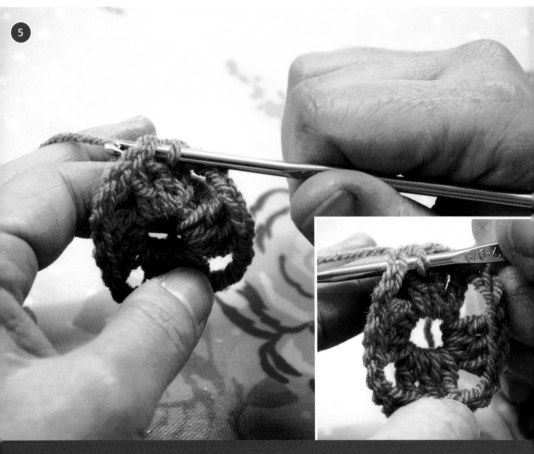

5. Working anti clockwise, slip stitch 3 times across to the next chain space, (or corner space).

6. Work 3 chains (counts as 1st treble).

7. Work 2 more trebles into this corner chain space, 3 chains, and 3 more trebles into same space.

8. Work every corner like this, then 1 chain between sets of trebles.
Slip stitch to close the round.

Granny Square changing colour...

1. Hold the end of the yarn as if it were attached to the granny square and put your fingers in position.

2. Push the hook through any chain space and pull the yarn back through.

3. Chain 3 (counts as first treble), and continue as before.

4. Remember: 3 trebles, 3 chains, 3 trebles in every corner space.

5. One chain between and sets of 3 trebles into the side spaces.

Chapter 5

Bunting
Decreasing...

1. Chain 25.

2. Push hook through 2nd chain from hook, draw the yarn back through but don't finish the stitch.

3. Repeat in the next stitch.

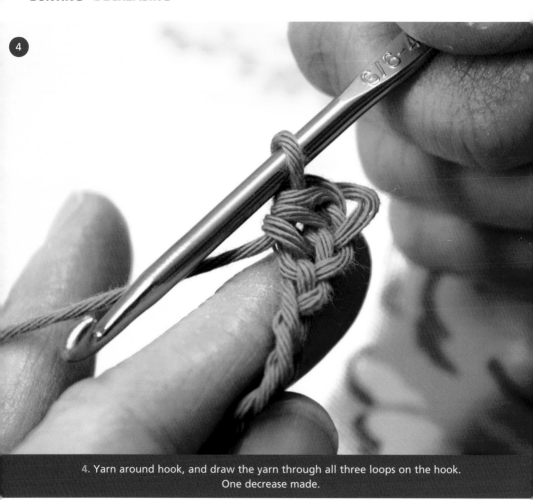

4. Yarn around hook, and draw the yarn through all three loops on the hook.
One decrease made.

5. Repeat this row, remembering to work the turning chain at the end, until 3 stitches remain, yarn round hook to close.

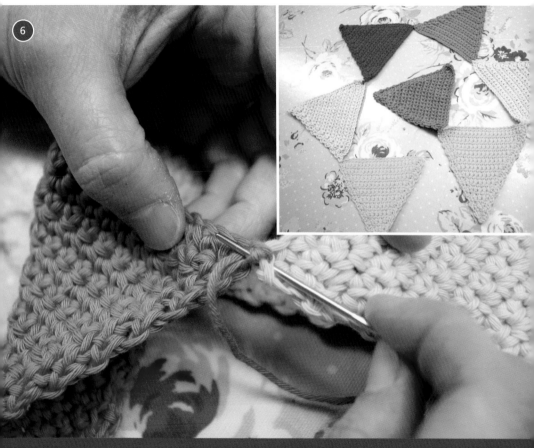

6. Sew each triangle together at the top edges.
The right side will have the chains at the top facing you.

Chapter 6.

Increasing

1. Work one double crochet.

2. Work another double crochet into the same stitch.

Working in the Round...

1. Chain 6 and slip stitch in the 1st stitch to close the ring.

2. Work 12 dc into the ring and close with slip stitch.

3. Work 2 chains; then work 2 dc into every stitch and ss to close, (24sts).

4. Work 2 chains. *Work 1 dc in next stitch, 2 dc in next stitch. Repeat from * all the way round. ss to close, (36sts).

⑤

5. Next round: work 2dc, then *1dc in each of next 2 sts, 2dc in next st*, repeat from * to * to the end.
Next round: work 2dc, then *1dc in each of next 3 sts, 2dc in next st*, repeat from * to * to the end.
Continue increasing every round in this way.

Magic Ring...

1. Hold the yarn, tail towards you. Wind it round your 3 fingers and cross over.

2. There will be two loops around your fingers.

3. Insert the hook under the first loop and hook the second loop.

4. Pull the yarn under and twist your hand like this.

5. Hook the second loop again.

6. Then pull through.

7. You now have a loop to work into.

8. Work into the centre of the loop.

9. Then work a dc as before.

Chapter 7

Crochet Basket

1. Make a magic ring. Work 6 dc into the ring. Pull ring closed and slip stitch to close the round.

2. Chain 2. Work 2 dc in every stitch all the way to round to end. ss to close.

3. Chain 2. Work 1 dc in 1st stitch, 2 dc in 2nd stitch – all the way to end. From now on work in a spiral, so place a marker here, then continue increasing as before until you have 6 rounds.

4. Next round: dc in the back strand of every dc to create an edge.

5. Work 4 more rounds with no increasing to create the side.

6. Next round: make two handles by working 10 chains, missing 5 dc and attaching in the 6th dc along with a slip stitch. Work 13 dc in next 13 stitches and repeat the handle on the other side. dc to end.

7. Work dc into the handle space as required.

8. Join the yarn back to the basket again, and dc to the next handle. Work the 2nd handle as before. dc to end, fasten off and tie in ends neatly.

Chapter 8.

Sewing Up
Oversewing...

1. Hold wrong sides of square together and secure yarn at beginning.

2. Insert the needle into the outer edge of both squares from the back to the front.

3. Repeat to end.

Using Chain (Slip Stitch)...

1. Holding the wrong sides together, hold the yarn as if it were attached, and insert the hook into the outer edges of both squares.

2. Pull the yarn back through and chain one.

3. Insert the hook into the next two stitches and pull the yarn back through.

4. pull the yarn through the loop on the hook like a slip stitch. Repeat to end.

Double Crochet Sewing Together

1. Insert the hook into the next stitch...

2. ...and pull through.

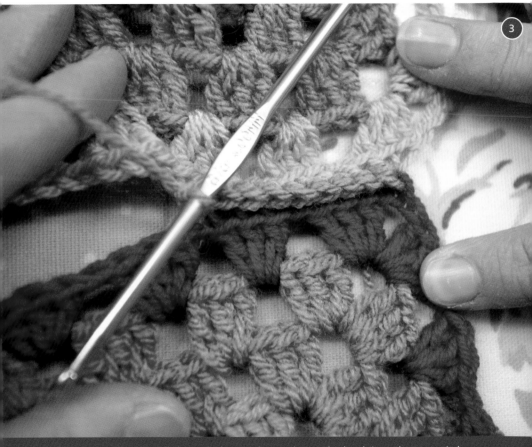

3. Yarn round hook, pull through the two loops, insert the hook into the next stitch and repeat to end.

Chapter 9

Edging

1. Join the yarn to the work in any chain space and ch1.

2. Dc into the top of every treble and one into every chain space.

3

3. Work 1 dc into the top of every stitch all the way round, working 3 dc into every corner space and 1 dc into every space along each side. Work to the end and fasten off neatly.

Picot edging...

1. Join yarn to the work. ch 2, ss into the base of the same stitch.

2. Dc into next 2 stitches, ch2, ss in base of same stitch
Repeat this all the way round, ss to close and sew in ends neatly.

Design & Artwork: ALEX YOUNG

Photography: CHLOE HARDWICK

Published by: DEMAND MEDIA LIMITED

Publisher: JASON FENWICK

Written by: CLARE DAVIES